How Not to Be a Dick

How Not to Be a Dick

An Everyday Etiquette Guide

Meghan Doherty

ZEST BOOKS
MINNEAPOLIS

www.zestbooks.net
Created and produced by Zest Books, Minneapolis

© 2013 Meghan Doherty

Zest Books™
An imprint of Lerner Publishing Group, Inc.
241 First Avenue North
Minneapolis, MN 55401 USA

Young Adult Nonfiction / Humor / General
Library of Congress control number: 2013937668
ISBN: 978-1-936976-02-7
Cover design: Meghan Doherty
Interior design: Marissa Feind

Manufactured in the United States of America
5-49444-26247-7/13/2020

HOW NOT TO BE A DICK AGREEMENT

This is to certify that I, _____,
resident of _____ in the State of _____,
will do everything in my power to avoid behaving like a dick.
Further, I will actively encourage others to avoid dickish
behavior. In order to avoid this, I will:

1.   Respect others.
2.   Be considerate.
3.   Listen.
4.   Communicate clearly.
5.   Treat everyone as an individual.
6.   Empathize.
7.   See the big picture.
8.   Value caring and sharing.
9.   Take responsibility for my actions and feelings.
10. Help others.

I pledge to use the tools and techniques provided in this book
to help make the world a less dickish place.

_____   _____

Book Owner   Date

Table of Contents

INTRODUCTION

Throughout history, there have been dicks. The kind of people who have the power to ruin even the nicest day. The kind of people who, when you're just enjoying a soothing cup of hot coffee in the morning, rush in, knock that coffee all over your favorite sweater, and don't even stop to help, much less apologize!

Dicks don't stop to consider how their attitudes, actions, and words affect other people. Dicks are, as a rule, selfish and thoughtless. They take out their fears, frustrations, insecurities, and ignorance on others. Dicks have been the cause of wars, snide *New Yorker* articles, and upsetting comments on cute cat blogs for as long as anyone can remember. That bully from grade school, that boss who promoted his fraternity brother over you, that kid in seventh grade who mocked your lisp—all dicks!

Nice one, Einstein!

To be totally honest, we can all be dicks at times. We can all get caught up in our own world, forget about everyone else, and start acting like dicks. We all have bad days, and we all make mistakes, even when we mean well. What can you do?

It's not easy being this perfect.

Here's what: Remember that we're all in it together. Remember to take a breath and think of those around you. Not being a dick can be hard. It takes work and practice. That's where this book can help! No matter what situation you find yourself in—attending a party, using the bathroom, sitting on the bus, taking a midterm, having a picnic, or just talking to someone you're really into—this book has the advice you need to not be a dick.

So without further ado, let's get cracking on creating a new, improved, non-dickish you!

CHAPTER 1
In Relationships

First, a Note About You

The first rule of not being a dick to others is: Don't be a dick to yourself. If you're vicious to yourself, you're probably going to be vicious to others, and if you're vicious to others, other people will be vicious to you. So don't walk around hating yourself or being a Negative Nancy. That doesn't help anyone.

Let's say you just went shopping and you bought an awesome new jacket. You like it so much that you don't want to take it off, so you keep it on even after you come indoors. Some people might find that unusual and ask you why you're wearing a jacket inside.

Why are you wearing your jacket inside?

What's it to you?

How do you react? If you feel insecure about yourself and your fashion choices, you might become defensive.

But if someone doesn't appreciate your style sensibility, let your own positivity prevail. Be proud of who you are and stand up for the choices you make.

If you want to wear your jacket inside, then wear your jacket inside. If some people think they can survive without a nice heavy jacket, best of luck to them when the long winter comes.

Comparing Yourself to Others

It's easy to focus on our own problems and shortcomings. If we're feeling bored or unhappy, we can't hide that reality from ourselves, whereas it's very difficult to see what other people are trying to keep under wraps. So upon seeing a boy playing ping-pong, you might think: "My life's so boring and dull. I'm so unhappy. If only I could play ping-pong like that boy, things would be different." There are a lot of nice things in the world and a lot of smiling people, but if you dwell too much on what you don't have, it's easy to feel inadequate.

The thing is, the other person could be thinking the same thing about you!

We don't really have any idea what's going on in another person's life. What looks great from the outside might not be so great on the inside.

Comparing yourself to others distracts you from focusing on yourself and what really matters to you. We have to define success for ourselves and appreciate our own talents. We have to find satisfaction in our own growth and achievements. After all, even when someone seems to have it all—with a hit TV show, piles of money, veins filled with tiger blood, and a goddess on each elbow— deep down, that person might be

depressed, flailing, and on the brink of an epic meltdown. Even those who "have it all" are missing things, too.

Remember: Success doesn't always bring happiness, and happiness isn't always easy to spot.

Body Image

The world is a big, huge, enormous place covered with billions and billions of people. But guess what? You're totally unique! Dystopian future cloning technologies aside, you're the only version of you there will ever be. Embrace it! Nobody is perfect! So don't worry about your so-called imperfections. Imagine what would happen if some future version of yourself traveled back through time to talk to you today.

How embarrassing is that? Instead of obsessing over your latest pimple, do something positive! Join a Sunday-afternoon kickball league, write that graphic novel you've been talking about, or really apply yourself at next year's science fair.

Your Feelings

Feelings are the mind's (and heart's) way of telling us something we need to know—like that we love someone or that spiders are creepy and evil. But sometimes we don't know why we feel the way we do. Sometimes, our emotions seem totally out of proportion to whatever caused them.

fig. 1　　　fig. 2　　　fig. 3

That's a sign we need to look more closely at what's going on. Don't ignore or dismiss your feelings, or you might end up doing something you regret. For instance, say you're at a friend's party. Everyone is having a great time, but you're not.

Maybe you blame the host's dog, who keeps staring at you with those big puppy eyes but who runs away every time you try to pet him. But is the dog really the problem? Take some time to examine why you feel the way you do.

First, *identify* how you feel.

Next, look for possible *causes* for your feelings.

Then, *understand* the connection.

Perhaps an upset stomach makes me cranky, not that stupid dog.

Finally, try to *solve* the problem in an active way.

I think I need to go for an evening constitutional to aid my digestion. I'll be back and ready to party in a bit!

If you stuff your difficult emotions into a little box and lock them up, you'll never figure out what's making you unhappy. You'll keep experiencing those negative emotions because you won't be interacting with the real problem. And sure, working through your emotions

I think I got to the root of your problem. It was definitely the cheese log you had for dinner.

I knew it!

can take a lot of time and energy (and perhaps a few visits to a professional therapist), but you're worth it! If you don't have enough money for a doctor, find a friend to talk to. It can make all the difference.

Honesty Is the Best Policy

Without honesty, none of the strategies described in this book are going to get you very far. Of course, being honest with yourself is easier said than done. (It would be dishonest not to admit that.) Still, don't you know deep down when you're pretending to be someone you're not? Or when you are just putting on a show to impress others? If we're pretending to be something just so people will like us, that's setting ourselves up for trouble. It takes a lot of energy to keep that show up 24/7.

Plus, if you overstate your talents, you'll only look foolish later.

Maybe you want to be a kung fu master, like this young lady. But if you aren't there quite yet, don't pretend to be.

Admit that you're still learning. People will understand because —think about it—they're probably in the process of learning something, too. If you don't know something, don't be afraid to ask someone who might know. People are naturally attracted to those who are curious and humble and who seek to improve themselves (whether that involves hand-to-hand combat or not).

When It Comes to Others

The single most important thing to remember in dealing with other people is: Everyone you meet is an individual and should be treated accordingly. So put yourself in the other person's shoes—and always get permission from everyone in your video before posting it on YouTube.

Making Generalizations

It's impossible to go through life (not to mention any given day) without making some assumptions. The important thing to remember, however, is that assumptions are just guesses. Even if they're not flat-out wrong, they are still usually incomplete.

Assumptions are conclusions based on what we don't know, rather than what we *do*. As a result, our assumptions tend to say more about what we believe than about the people we are assuming things about. This young lady might have bangs, wear DIY fashions, and live in a city, but that doesn't mean she can pickle her own cucumbers.

And this young man may be a small-town football hero, but that doesn't mean that he's into cheerleaders.

Stereotypes based on race, gender, sexuality, nationality, or anything else—*Star Trek* fans, "dirty" hippies, professional athletes, and so forth—mislead us when we come into contact with individuals. Sure, stereotypes might be based on a kernel of truth (most Trekkies *are* awesome), but that shouldn't stop us from being open to understanding the unique person standing right in front of us.

After all, one young man might fancy cheese in a can, but does that mean every young man likes cheese in a can?

People of Different Cultural Backgrounds

The world has more cultures than you can shake a stick at. It's a vast place filled with many different people with many different customs. And that's a good thing!

Everyone has something different to bring to the table. Those differences are what make our world such an interesting place. Vive la différence!

People of Different Sexual Orientations

We can't help who we love. That's what the scientific evidence suggests, and that's what our hearts tell us, too.

Just because one person is straight doesn't mean that everyone else has to be. And just because one person is not straight also doesn't mean that everyone else has to be. There's room on this spinning globe for all of us, so follow the Golden Rule and treat people of different sexual orientations as you would want to be treated.

People of Different Religious Faiths

Of course, along with all the other differences that make our world go round is the fact that people hold a wide variety of religious and spiritual beliefs. Questions about how we got here and what we're supposed to be doing with our time on Earth are an essential aspect of nearly every spiritual tradition.

Religions rely on belief for answers to many of these essential (and existential) questions. And believing in an idea is kind of like falling in love with a person—it just seems right, even if

we can't fully explain it. That's okay, but it can lead to disagreements. We don't have to all believe the same thing. Allow people to have their own beliefs, even if those beliefs are different from your own. We'll all get along better if we're free to explain the whys and wherefores of our beliefs without feeling patronized or bullied. And that's the whole point, right?

Having pets makes it easier to watch *Game of Thrones*.

People of Different Abilities

Treating people who are disabled goes back to the Golden Rule, "Treat others as you would want to be treated." Just because some are born hard of hearing, for instance, doesn't mean that they don't want the same things out of life that everyone else does or couldn't perform many, if not all, of the same tasks. Don't make assumptions about what people with disabilities can or cannot do, just as you wouldn't make such assumptions about anyone else.

Another point to remember is what might be considered a "disability" by an outsider may very well be a nonissue for that person—or a point of pride.

Young People

Unless you were just born this very second (in which case, congratulations on your incredible reading comprehension skills!), there are a lot of people who are younger than you—and probably less experienced as a result. But even though you may have seen more of the world, that doesn't mean that they don't have knowledge to share or have a valid perspective. Maybe you've been through a million romantic breakups, but you shouldn't negate others' experiences just because it's their first time.

Help that youngster by sharing your experience, but also by asking questions. This is the most useful way to help others learn from their experiences.

Who knows? You might gain something, too. Perhaps a new strategy for dealing with heartache or just a new and improved sense of how fast kids grow up.

The Elderly

Guess what? There will also always be people older than you, too! Hurray for aging! Just note: Older often means wiser, but not always. Life on Earth takes its toll, and some have paid larger tolls than others.

Don't assume that just because people are older that they are also "out of touch." If they've earned the right to a senior discount at the movie theater, cut them some slack.

Aging is hard, but experience brings wisdom. So listen up every chance you get. Those who have gone before you can be your guide to the life ahead of you.

If all goes well and you make it to old age, you'll be facing the same serious challenges they are. Wouldn't you hope for an understanding, kind, young-ish person to help you and listen to your awesome stories?

IN CONVERSATION

Whoever you are, wherever you're going, and whatever you want to do, you're going to need to talk to people. How else are you going to communicate? With passive-aggressive post-its?

No thanks. Just use your words. The words you use and the way you talk to people says a lot about who you are. They also help determine whether or not people will listen to you.

Greeting Others

Whenever you encounter some-one—whether crossing an ice floe in Antarctica or just passing on a crowded street—it's always polite to say, "Hello." This is often followed by, "How are you?"

This simple acknowledgment of another person is Politeness 101. Use it often!

Initiating a Conversation

Sometimes you might want to say more than hello. You might have an issue to discuss, or you might see someone that you'd like to get to know better. In these cases, make sure the person isn't already busy or engaged in another conversation. Don't just butt in and start talking. That's rude!

Interrupting not only derails the original conversation, it also makes you look like a total dick! So play it cool.

Seriously, just wait your turn. Stand close but not too close, and eventually the talkers will get the hint and pause, allowing you to introduce yourself.

Congratulations, you just started a conversation! Keep practicing!

Once you've introduced yourself, immediately address the subject you want to discuss. However, if the person is a stranger, take things more slowly than you would with a friend or acquaintance. Start by asking a question about that person or perhaps by commenting on something you can both see in the surrounding area.

Once the conversation is started, you can springboard into more in-depth topics. Or you can get to the point.

Personal Space

When we talk with someone, our bodies say a lot. It's important  to maintain proper personal space. Allow an arm's length distance between you and the person you're speaking with, aka "the interlocutor." This gives your interlocutor some breathing room. People are more at ease and communicate better when they don't feel hemmed in or threatened.

Hovering is a sure-fire way to make someone feel instantly uncomfortable. It's easy to do if you're not on the lookout. How do you know when you're too close?

Hovering happens when:

You look over someone's shoulder.

You stand just behind or next to someone.

You stand over someone who is sitting.

Standing while someone is sitting sends a message about who is in charge of the conversation. It creates a real power imbalance.

Eye Contact

If you're talking with someone you're really attracted to, you might be tempted to take this opportunity to appreciate all aspects of his or her physical appeal. A word of advice, however: Save it for later! During a conversation, take care to maintain eye contact. This communicates that you're a sincere, respectful individual who is genuinely interested in what the other person is saying.

By staring at areas other than the face, you may make the other person uncomfortable. It's hard not to notice someone looking at you in an inappropriate way.

Give others the respect of looking at them in the eye when talking.

Asking Questions

Questions are an essential part of any conversation, particularly with someone you're trying to get to know better. They keep things dynamic. Or at least, they *can* if you ask the right ones. Avoid questions that require only a "yes" or "no" answer.

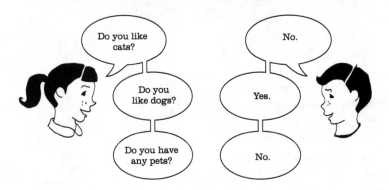

Instead, try to ask open-ended questions. These demonstrate an engaged mind, since they ask us to *think* and maybe get off our established script. As questions lead to answers (which lead to more questions, and so on and so on), you will discover what truly makes people tick and get a better sense of whether or not you really want to be spending any more time with them.

Oh cool, what was the cheese log tour like?

Active Listening

Listening sounds easy enough, but it can take real work. Words have to be deciphered and understood. It takes considerable effort and energy to stay focused while someone is offering an in-depth account of his or her deepest passion.

I mean, you call that a trike race? I have been racing trikes in Europe, and we topped speeds of three blocks per minute. THREE BLOCKS!

When in conversation, show that you're listening by asking focused questions. Demonstrate your interest by repeating back some of the most provocative points and then engaging in some new way. It may be hard, but it can have a huge impact on the quality of the overall conversation—and on the other person's opinion of you.

Three blocks, impressive! Have you raced in the states at all?

Actively Not Listening

Even when we *are* listening, one bad habit we often fall into is the stock response. We overuse reaction words such as "right," "okay," "yeah," and "uh huh." Repeatedly making these sounds gives the impression we're not actually interested. They also interrupt the flow of the other person's story.

Right, right, right, okay. I know. Yeah. Right, right. I know.

Convey active listening with an expression of concentration and wait for the person to pause before responding. Avoid adding interjections after every sentence.

After all, patterned responses often provide us with the wrong word at the wrong time.

Sometimes as we're listening, ideas occur to us that have little to no relationship to the conversation. What's on our mind may seem more important than what the other person is saying, but it's still rude to change topics too abruptly.

At best, this makes it look like you don't value the conversation; at worst, it makes it seem like you don't value the *person*. So even when you are listening and want to bring up something new, take care to provide a smooth transition.

And if you miss something, instead of pretending that you got it, just ask the person to repeat what you missed.

Talking About Yourself

When having a conversation with someone, avoid talking about yourself too much. Of course, no one is better qualified to talk about you than you, but by the same token, the other person generally won't be as interested in you as you think. To avoid disappointment (and the reputation of being self-centered), continually turn the conversation back to the other person. How can you tell if you're hijacking the conversation? If it looks like this:

Remember: Be courteous and share the conversation! Your turn to speak will come . . . eventually.

Acting Cool

When your turn to talk does comes up, be yourself! Don't tailor your identity to the other person's expectations.

The real you is way more interesting! Besides, it's too much work to keep up a façade. Be honest about who you are and what you're looking for, and you'll attract people who appreciate you for you. Be upfront about your hobbies and interests.

TMI

Okay, back up for a second. That advice about total honesty doesn't apply to everything. When meeting someone for the first time, try to avoid personal topics, such as breakups, sexual liaisons, rashes, gossip about common friends, and monologues about how your parents ruined your life.

I need someone to make out with me.

Suzy is awful! Look at those shoes.

I know I want to talk about my recent breakup, but instead, I'll have a conversation we can both partake in.

Before speaking, think: "If I typed this in an email and sent it to my entire address book, would I be embarrassed?" If so, save the conversation for a more intimate setting. It's great to be honest, but show some tact and discretion.

Humor

Humor is a great addition to any conversation. Everyone enjoys a good laugh. Laughter brings us closer together. However, remember that not everyone finds the same things amusing.

The better question is what was she doing out of the kitchen! HAHA.

Jokes that belittle others or trade in stereotypes—particularly if they make fun of some aspect of the person you're with—can backfire. A bad joke is one thing, but intolerance is no laughing matter.

So stay away from jokes based on racial, ethnic, cultural, or gender stereotypes. And if someone makes a tasteless joke, let that person know that kind of humor is wrong and only peddled by dicks and stand-up comics looking to express their inner regret.

If you hear a joke that isn't based on hate or stereotypes, don't be afraid to pass it on!

Asking for Someone's Phone Number

Few things are more anxiety producing than asking for some-one else's phone number (because rejection stinks!). Despite all the effort you've put into active listening, the person might still say no.

Of course, people might have a good reason for not giving you their phone number, and it might have nothing to do with you. Maybe they're in a relation-ship, or maybe they just want to enjoy a night with their friends.

So, just accept that things might not turn out, and that's okay! There are tons of fish in the sea. If you react with anger, it will only make things worse.

And if the person says yes, then ask politely to exchange phone numbers so that you both share the calling power!

Ending a Conversation

All good things must come to an end, and that goes for conversations, too. To avoid any awkwardness, be as upfront as possible. Let the other person finish his or her sentence, then nip things off firmly.

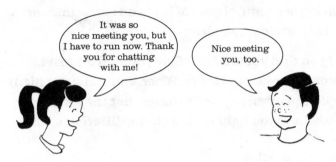

If you want to go because the other person has said something truly offensive or won't stop looking at you inappropriately, don't descend to her level.

If someone really is being a dick, you don't want to prolong things or provoke even worse dickish behavior.

IN A FIGHT

If you spend a lot of time around people—whether in class, at your job, in social circles, or in a relationship—disagreements and squabbles are bound to happen. Fighting is a natural part of life, and sometimes arguments help clear the air.

So if you find yourself in a fight, don't fret! Just be careful not to get carried away. When emotions run high, people can often say or do things that they will later regret. *How* you fight makes all the difference.

Pick Your Battles

When you find yourself in a disagreement with someone, first take a breath and ask yourself, "Is this fight worth it?"

Sometimes, the subject of an argument isn't worth fighting over, and the best strategy is to agree to disagree. Each person's point of view can be valid. If you try to convince other people that they're wrong, you run the risk of saying something mean and making the argument personal.

Consider whether what you are saying is really contributing to a constructive discussion.

Remember, you have to pick your battles. A canine POTUS ("The 45th President of the United States, Eddie Crane!") may be an incredibly adorable idea, but is it really worth fighting about?

In the end, what's more important: winning the argument or saving your relationship?

See the Other Side

When emotions flare and tem-
pers are high, it's hard to think
straight, let alone say what you
mean—especially when you're
both shouting each other down.
Try to allow the other person to
finish, no matter how right or
wrong you think he is. Take a
moment to try to see his side of
things. You might learn something.

The other person will probably say some things
that you do not agree with, but now is not the
time to interrupt. After all, just think how
frustrating it is when someone interrupts you.
It can often cause us to boil over.

Think Before You Speak

Once the other person has finished, it's your turn to have the
floor—but wait! Once again, take
a breath and think before you
speak. The other party may have
said some hurtful things, and you
might want to return the favor.

But won't that only make things
worse? Count to ten slowly, and let
yourself calm down. Then start by
recognizing the larger perspective.
Not only does this let the person know
you care, but taking the high road is the
best way to get an argument back on track.

Apologize for Any Wrongdoing

Then, consider if the other person has said anything even remotely accurate at all. Remember, any relationship is a two-way street, and you probably played some part in this fight. Is there any area you can recognize where you were in the wrong? If so, take the time to acknowledge that fact.

Take Responsibility for Your Feelings

Let's just say, for example, that the other person has said some mean things that have made you very angry.

Those angry feelings are your responsibility. Before you can discuss the issue at hand, you have to express your feelings—preferably with a well-crafted "I" statement. After all, that young lady isn't saying you're a bad person. She is just expressing her personal opinion about the flavor of your logs.

If you attack the other person, that will put her on the defensive. Only you can control how you feel. So focus on solving the problem without letting emotions get in the way. That's the best way to find a solution that will work for everyone.

CHAPTER 2
At Home

LIVING WITH OTHERS

Being a good roommate doesn't mean you have to be perfect. It just requires that you pay attention, act considerately, do your fair share, and don't lose your temper when someone else forgets to do some of those things. But whether you're living with parents, siblings, friends, roommates, animals, or all of the above, there are a few basic rules that it also helps to bear in mind.

Mind Your Manners

The words *please* and *thank you* are like magical fairy dust. They give us the power to brighten someone's day. When living with others, let them know you appreciate everything they do.

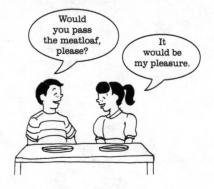

But be careful. Too much praise can make people self-conscious and suspicious of your motives. So don't overdo it. Sincerity is the key!

Respectful Behavior

It's not only what you say, it's what you do that counts. Please and thank you don't mean much if your behavior is rude or disrespectful.

So, first things first: Always treat your living quarters with respect. If it's not your name on the lease, you may think you can't be sued or evicted. But just because you didn't buy the couch doesn't mean you won't have to pay for it if you damage it.

Also, act respectfully toward those you live with. Minimize your impact on others and keep things in order. So don't clang around in the kitchen while your roommate is asleep. That goes double if you're living with your parents.

If you're living at home, it's time to double-down on politeness and to be very conservative when it comes to your "sense of decency." Your parents don't want to see you hitting on the girl from down the street.

Communicate

No matter who you live with, don't treat them like pieces of furniture. Talk to them! Show some common courtesy and let them know if you're going to have an overnight guest or if you're going away on a trip. After all, if they don't know you're hiking the Appalachian trail, they're likely to assume anything!

Just as important, meet with roommates (or your parents) regularly to discuss your schedule and air any grievances. Those you live with may be silently seething about your behavior, but you won't know unless you ask. Most of all, if something you're doing might affect the household, let the household know.

Chip In

Naturally, in a roommate situation, everyone has to pay his or her fair share of the rent. "Chipping in" covers all the other things the household shares: cleaning products, toilet paper and tissues, milk and other groceries, and so on. Be proactive about this: If you use something, help pay for it, or take turns buying more at the grocery store.

Of course, times are hard. Maybe you don't have any extra money for the little things. You can still make up for it in other ways—by doing more of the chores, for instance, or trading a skill you have.

I'll balance your checkbook if I can have some of your ketchup.

Maybe you don't have any money at all, and so maybe you're living with your parents. (That's okay!) In the meantime, pitch in without forcing your parents to ask, and they will respect you for the considerate person that you've become.

Also, consider getting a job. Even if jobs are scarce, at least submit some applications. Start building up that résumé! Even a temporary job at the burger shack is a positive first step.

The more you can show your parents that you're not mooching off of them, the less tension there will be between you.

I'm going camping this weekend with my friends from school! Love you bunches!

AT THE TABLE

Eating is a necessary part of human existence. Food gives us the energy we need to live, and usually it tastes good! But whether you prepared the meal or not, here are some mealtime basics.

Chew with Your Mouth Closed

Not only does chewing with your mouth open sound disgusting, it looks barbaric. There are other ways to show the cook how much you liked the food.

Treat your lips like a cabin door in winter: Keep them closed.

Be Considerate

No matter how good the food is or how hungry you are, take your time while eating, sit up straight, and avoid slurping.

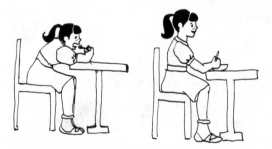

If you find yourself making noise, slow down.

Not every meal agrees with us. These internal arguments can ruin a meal.

Cover your mouth if you must burp, and excuse yourself from the table if you need to pass gas.

Take Off Your Hat

Wearing a hat shades your eyes and makes it look like you don't want to be there. By removing your hat, you show respect for the people you are eating with.

Do Not Spit

. . . on food to claim it.

It's gross. And it's cheating.

In the Bathroom

Bathrooms are a sensitive area and often a taboo topic. What takes place in the bathroom is natural, though. Don't ignore your body or its functions. But let's make sure to keep it clean.

Close the Lid

No matter whether you're a girl or a boy, always close the lid before you flush the toilet. When the toilet flushes, all that swirling water can spray up. That's a great way to get a stye in the eye!

And a great way to start distrusting your toothbrush.

Ehhh.

The solution is simple: Close that lid before you flush. Send your waste away quietly. It's so easy to do!

fig. 1   fig. 2

Wash Your Hands

If you are an employee, there's usually a sign that you must wash your hands after you go to the bathroom. Here is some more good advice: Treat yourself like an employee of life! Wash your hands every time you use the bathroom, whether you're at work or not. This is the way to avoid food poisoning and unpleasant nicknames.

Spend a full twenty seconds washing, surgeon style. Wash front and back and get under the nails. Don't stop until you've sung the "Happy Birthday" song twice in a row!

Shower Etiquette

If you live with other people, keep your showers short and sweet. Take only the time you need to get clean. Don't linger while singing into your scrub brush. Conserve hot water, which both your roommates and the environment will appreciate. After showering, wipe down the tub and remove any hair.

Leave the bathroom clean for the next person who uses it. Do not throw hair on wall.

Pee in the Toilet, Not the Shower

The water is running, it's comfortable, you need to go, and you think, "Hey, it's all going down the same pipes, anyway . . ." No! Stop right there. Think before you pee. Do you want your shower to smell like urine? Is that really what you want to be discussing at your next roommate meeting?

I will not pull a George Costanza.

If you get the urge while showering, get out and do it in the toilet. Better to have some water on the floor than urine in the shower.

During Housecleaning

Chores may be unpleasant, but they sure are necessary. It's hard to relax when the place where you live looks and smells like a zoo. So do your part. Work with your roommates to give your house a good scrub.

Pick Up After Yourself

The easiest way to keep chores manageable—and limit your roommates' irritation—is to always pick up after yourself. Put things back where they belong after you use them. Don't leave your unopened mail on the floor and books all over the place. Tackle a mess when it's small. It just saves energy.

If you spill crumbs on the living room carpet, vacuum them up immediately. This keeps them from being tracked all over, and your roommates will appreciate not stepping on stale potato chips when they watch TV.

Do the Dishes

When it comes to roommate harmony and household cleanliness, perhaps nothing is more important than doing your dishes right after use.

If you use all the pots and pans to make your dinner and then don't wash them, this forces your roommates to clean up your mess before they can make their own dinner. No one appreciates that. Furthermore, loose-lying food attracts insects and mice.

Bathroom Maintenance

Bathrooms get dirty fast, but follow some everyday maintenance rules and yours won't lead to roommate wars!

After using the bathroom, review your work areas (so to speak). In the morning, after you've finished your toilette, put your products away, leave the counter clean, and wipe off the sink. (Spare your roommates from encountering the morning loogie you hocked up.)

As before, don't forget to sweep the hair from the tub drain.

Communication and Chore Routines

The best way to create a happy household is to set up a chore routine or a chore chart. Maybe your parents did this when you were a kid. Well, it still works! People are happier when they work together and know what's expected of them. However, if you find your roommates are not partaking in chores, first try talking with them directly. They may not realize that they aren't doing their fair share.

Make a conversation of it! Avoid passive-aggressive notes, or making personal attacks. This will just cause unnecessary tension.

Rewards and Trades

Everyone's share of household duties doesn't have to be perfectly equal. Consider making trades to ensure that no one feels taken advantage of. If someone is going to be cleaning more often, give them a break somewhere else.

After a hard day of cleaning the house together, it's often a good idea to reward yourselves in a way that shows appreciation for everyone's efforts.

Around Your Neighbors

Neighbors can be great and neighbors can be terrible, but you just never know which it's going to be until after you move in. The one thing you can depend on? You. How you handle it makes all the difference.

Good Fences Make Good Neighbors

Just because someone lives next to you—whether in the next house or in an adjacent apartment—it doesn't automatically make you friends.

That's okay. Give your neighbors space to live their own lives. If you're meant to become friends, you will!

Home is a place to relax. If you try to force friendship on your neighbors, they may resent it, and once you get to know them, you may find you don't like them anyway. Do you really want to spend the rest of your time dodging each other's hellos? Take it slow and give your relationship time to flourish!

Throwing a House Party

When planning a house party, be sure to let your neighbors know so that they can be fully prepared. That way, if they don't like loud noises, they'll have time to make other plans. They will also appreciate that you're making an effort to minimize any inconveniences.

Definitely come along if you'd like. I have an extra set of constable gear, so no need to bring anything!

Naturally, everyone loves a party. Invite your neighbors, too. They'll be grateful that you thought of them.

Most important, if your neighbors aren't attending, don't abuse their patience. Keep parties from running too late, particularly on a school or work night.

Then, when the party is over, make sure guests continue to use their inside voices when leaving your house or apartment. You may be in your neighbor's position one day, and you will appreciate the courtesy.

WOOOOOO!!

WHEN INVITING GUESTS

Whether you are planning a killer bash or simply an intimate evening with one or two close friends, you'll need to keep your roommates in mind as well.

Ask First

If you live with others, don't forget you have to share the space. Your roommates or your parents may have their own plans for the same night. But whatever they are doing, they won't appreciate coming home to find an impromptu party going on.

Oh, hi.

At minimum, inform your roommates or your parents of any plans in advance.

Hey, I was thinking of having my poker buddies over for a little bit tonight.

For bigger gatherings or parties, ask your roommates' or your parents' permission first before setting the date. That shows respect for their lives, too.

Would it be cool to have a rager this weekend?

This is particularly important if the event will impact others in a serious way.

Just like your neighbors, don't forget to invite your roommates to join in! When everybody is involved in the fun, everybody wins!

The Extended Sleepover

When hosting a sleepover, be considerate of your roommates and any other people who share your space. Staying up late and making loud noises will disrupt their lives (and sleeping patterns). So try to keep any noise or disruptions to a minimum.

If you have a particular friend who attends a lot of your sleepover parties, try and split your time between your respective homes. That way, the other people you live with won't feel crowded and can get a good night's sleep at least half the time.

It's also important to make sure your guest respects your roommates' belongings. As a good host, you should provide your guest with access to toiletries and other items so they don't have to use your roommates' things.

CHAPTER 3
At School

In the Classroom

School is a great place to develop your abilities, try new things, and hone your social skills. It's also chockablock with trials and tribulations—making it a ripe terrain for dickishness of all sorts.

Respect Your Teacher

Here's your first lesson: Respect the teacher. Teachers are there to help us learn. They want us to succeed. They want us to succeed so much that they even went back to school to learn how to teach. That's dedication!

Teachers do very difficult and very important work that benefits our whole community. They deserve respect.

But whether you've got the best teacher ever or the sleepiest teacher ever, be an advocate for your own education. Talk to your teacher first if you foresee any problems, and if the teacher doesn't respond in a productive manner, consider speaking with a counselor, too.

Don't Make Excuses

Sometimes homework just doesn't get done. So what should you do when this happens?

Don't lie about it. Most likely, your teacher has already heard every excuse in the book. So don't waste your instructor's time. In fact, the reason something *didn't* get done doesn't really matter. What matters is what you do about it. Will you be honest and responsible? See if the teacher will let you make it up. At the very least, show you've learned your lesson, and don't let it happen again.

Getting Extra Help

Admittedly, the stress of school can be intense. You're balancing a lot of plates: nightly homework, major assignments every week, sports and band, learning new languages, and getting changed in a locker room. Meanwhile, your friends are texting every two minutes. The pressure is on—to be both academically successful and not a social loser!

It's easy to feel overwhelmed! If you find yourself having a difficult time, don't be afraid to seek help. That's what guidance counselors and academic advisors are for.

Together, you may be called to come up with a solution to scheduling problems, for instance. But even just venting your frustrations to a trained professional can be very reassuring and keep you from lashing out at friends or younger siblings.

Also, if you need more help in class, don't forget your teacher. Ask your instructor to tutor you after school or during their office hours. Whatever you need, don't be afraid to ask for help!

Cheating

Whether you're short on time or low on GPA, cheating is often tempting as a quick solution. Learning is hard, but peeking over a classmate's shoulder takes only a second. While most cheaters get caught eventually, "eventually" can take an awful long time. In the meantime, the cheater gets to enjoy looking like a hero.

But when praise and success aren't earned, they are harder to enjoy—because you know that they've been based on a lie.

When you cheat, no matter how you do it, you're presenting a false picture of who you are. You might succeed in the short term—say, winning the race at field day seven years in a row—but that won't get you anywhere in the long term.

Extracurricular Activities

School is the perfect place to try out new things. You get the chance to figure out what you like and what you don't like as well as what it's like to succeed and fail in front of the whole student body. Talk about a life lesson! So go for it!

Never again will you have so much equipment and so many resources at your disposal. Never again will you have so many coaches and games, and so many fields and stages to display your talents. Avail yourself of those opportunities! You might find that you're an excellent mathlete. Or a bowling kingpin.

Just remember to keep things in perspective. You can only do so much at once, so you may have to choose. And when it comes to competition, don't take winning and losing too seriously. Everyone likes to win, but everybody loses sometimes. When you lose, be sure to congratulate the winners on a job well done. You'll get 'em next time!

WHEN MAKING FRIENDS

At school, you're bound to make loads of friends. Some may remain your best friends forever, and some . . . not so much. If you're nervous, just remember: The best way to get along with your peers is to be yourself!

One surefire way to make friends is to join a group that interests you, like soccer or the AV club.

Maybe you can join a lunch table where others are playing a game that interests you.

Not everyone will share your interests, and many people might think you are weird or strange to have them, but that doesn't mean that you are not A-OK.

Even if only three people at school share your interests, find those people now. It stands to reason that if you like something, someone else likes it, too.

You may be outnumbered at the moment, but someday you'll see that the world is a big place, and it has lots of similar fish in it!

Cliques and Karma

Cliques are like the base unit of almost every school. Like atoms gathering into molecules, everyone forms into like-minded, easily identifiable masses, which has pluses and minuses.

On the one hand, cliques can help us express our identities and celebrate our interests and talents.

On the other hand, forming cliques can also be a way to exclude those we don't like so we can feel superior to them.

The paradox of this is that all cliques look down on some groups, and every clique is itself looked down on by others. Being in a group may sometimes help us feel superior, but that very identity

will be treated as inferior by someone else. Talk about a no-win situation!

So do yourself a favor and don't play this game. What goes around comes around, as they say. If you tease and exclude others, they (or someone else) will likely tease and exclude you. Whereas if you defend those who get teased, you will likely find others willing to defend you.

Put yourself in the other person's shoes. Wouldn't you appreciate someone sticking up for you?

Hey, you're being a dick. Back off.

Talking vs. Gossip

Talking with friends and gossiping about friends can look and sometimes sound the same, but they are very different. In short, talking is when we share our lives with each other in order to become closer and help each other. Gossiping is when we share negative things about someone else's life and do so with a negative purpose. Gossiping enables us to look down on people and distance ourselves from them. Unfortunately, gossip is a persistent and pernicious element of life at every age. Gossiping about celebrities may seem like fun, but not if you're the celebrity everyone's gossiping about!

In an ideal world, every time we heard anyone spreading malicious rumors, we would immediately abandon the conversation and walk away.

Gossiping is dumb. I'm out.

Gossip usually feeds on distance. We don't know celebrities, and so we feel free to mock them. Besides, they are public figures, and they asked for it, right? Maybe so, but that doesn't mean gossip doesn't do real harm, particularly when it happens in school and in the workplace. So think before you speak.

If you wouldn't say something to someone's face, don't say it at all. That goes double for texting and tweeting.

You may think you're talking in secret behind someone's back, but in this day and age, someone's probably recording or retweeting you. Everyone will eventually know who said what, so nip that nastiness in the bud.

Bullying

At its extreme, all this cliquish behavior can lead to bullying. Sometimes, like the line between gossip and talking, it can be difficult to differentiate casual joking from deliberate bullying. People may take offense when we think we were just kidding around and having a little fun!

Ultimately, bullying behavior is easy to spot: It's making fun of people and their interests in a way that belittles them. Typically, it's a lazy way to make ourselves feel superior. The only message it conveys is: "I'm better than you, and you don't deserve any respect." That's not right. We're all on this earth together!

If someone is hurt or takes offense at what we consider an "innocent joke," consider what the joke really said. Ask yourself: "Was I making fun of that person?"

Am I hurting someone?

If so, apologize. One of the worst things about bullying is that it ostracizes people. It makes them feel alone and undeserving of friends. No one wants to be singled out, made fun of, or physically hurt. That's why the Golden Rule is considered golden: It asks us to treat everyone as we ourselves would like to be treated.

fig. 1   fig. 2

Report Bullying

If you find yourself being bullied—
or see it happening to someone else—
report it to the school or a trusted
authority figure. Don't resign yourself to
that kind of behavior. Get help!

> I wanted to let you know that this is happening, and it's affecting me and my schoolwork.

Bullies are sometimes good at hiding their behavior.
Teachers and school officials may not realize what's
going on. Others might turn a blind eye, afraid to
recognize the harm that is being inflicted. By reporting the
issue, you bring it to the attention of those who can help. Once
the behavior is documented, it will be harder to deny. This also
helps officials determine if immediate intervention is necessary, or if the situation just needs to be monitored.

When we keep bullying to ourselves,
it can cause us to feel depressed or
isolated. Reach out to someone you
trust if you feel this way.

> There's someone being a dick to me at school, and I want to talk about it.

Even if nothing can be done
immediately, you can still take care
of yourself. If you can avoid the
bully or separate yourself from the
situation, that's sometimes the best
approach. Remember: Bullying says more about the person
doing the bullying than it does about you. It's admittedly
very difficult, but don't get caught up in the bully's drama.

AT THE DANCE

Whether your school hosts sock hops, formals, Sadie Hawkins dances, or only a year-end prom, there's nothing like a dance. It's one of the few school events that teaches the truly essential lessons of adulthood. Besides, whatever happens, you know that people will be talking about it the next day.

Different dances have different rules. Some rules are written and some are unwritten. Make sure you pay attention to both!

Asking Someone Out

The first time you ask someone to be your date will either be very exhilarating or very embarrassing. Either way, you'll never forget it (even if you'd like to).

How you make the request is vital to success. Timing and sincerity are key. Don't wait till the last minute, or someone might ask the person before you. However, make sure you've had at least one conversation with the person first.

Jimmy Jr. did say maybe. Ehhhhhh.

Make your request in person and speak from the heart, honestly and directly. Nothing is more romantic, and that's what it's all about! The other person may say no. But there's no shame in rejection—only slight embarrassment. You'll get over it.

Then again, having a date is rarely obligatory. If there's no one you want to ask, don't be afraid to go solo. You won't be alone!

How to Dress

Most schools have dress codes for dances. Read them carefully! You don't want to be turned away at the door because your "fashion statement" flouted some silly rule about hem height, exposed undergarments, or bare skin.

Don't forget that people are going to be taking pictures, often against backdrops of crepe paper and badly painted theme murals. Some things are harder to live down when there's visual evidence.

Make sure you're not the only one who loves your outfit—especially if you want to choose something outlandish. Definitely ask your friends for help, but be sure you're wearing what you want to wear and not just what everyone else is wearing!

Another thing to bear in mind is that your date—if you're bringing one—will be wearing clothes, too. If you attire yourself extravagantly, that might clash with your date's preference for nondescript understatement.

How to Dance

Dancing is supposed to be fun, but that can be hard when your body and your mind keep giving you different instructions. Don't worry too much about it though.

Just relax! Listen to the music and enjoy yourself.

CHAPTER 4

At Work

WHEN LOOKING FOR A JOB

Jobs pay money, and money pays the bills. That's just the way things work. It's not always easy, but it beats the alternative. (Because who wants to hunt wild game every day and then fend off large predators around the campfire every night?)

Just remember: Jobs are hard to get. And not every job is something you want to do your whole life. Mowing lawns and flipping burgers is great when you're young, but it's tough to stay on your feet all day when you get older.

Here's your nonfat mocha latte, son.

So don't just look for any job. Look for a job that will bring you happiness, some degree of security, and the satisfaction of being a contributing member of our society.

Applying for a Job

Before you apply for a job, consider what kind of job you'd like. There are many types of jobs in the world.

Then consider: Do your skills and experience match the needs of the job you want? If not, you might want to consider either gaining some skills or looking for a different kind of job.

Once you've found a job that seems like a good match, there are a few things you should bear in mind. First, it is extremely important not to lie or "fluff up" your résumé. Present your skills and experience honestly. In the interview, always be professional and polite.

Superhero of EVERYTHING!

If you're tempted to fudge what you know or have done, remember that this is just like cheating in school.

Like your teachers, employers would much rather know the truth about what you know and are capable of. They want to put you in a position where you will succeed. In that sense, they want what you want. (Plus, employee background checks are sure to turn up any real whoppers.)

Lying on a résumé or misrepresenting yourself in an interview can have dire consequences. It can hurt your eligibility for the position you're applying for, and it might even jeopardize your future job prospects as well.

Not everyone knows how to do everything, and that's okay. Turn any ignorance into an asset.

Show them that you can be a team player. Express your enthusiasm for all aspects of the job, no matter how tedious. Convince an employer of that, and you might join that enviable but often elusive group: the employed!

WHILE GETTING READY FOR WORK

Did you get a job? Good for you! Jobs are great! Here's everything you need to know about getting ready for a successful day in the workforce.

Before Beginning

Before you start each workday, make sure you get plenty of sleep and wake up with enough time to get ready at your own speed. You'll get enough stress at work. Don't start your day that way!

Instead, allow enough time to enjoy a hot beverage and a nutritious breakfast before heading out.

Proper Office Attire

When getting ready for work, choose clean, presentable clothes. Clothes should be lint free and comfortable. Make sure clothes are professional and not tight or constricting—loose, but not too revealing. Think about what others will be wearing. After all, you don't want clothes so comfortable they make those around you uncomfortable.

For instance, this outfit is perfect for the club.

But at most office jobs, it will just confuse people.

This outfit is perfect for an HBO series.

However, sitting might be difficult.

Save your high fashion for when you're out with your friends!

Personal Hygiene

Make sure to shower and brush your teeth every day. Maybe even more than once! Work is filled with lots of people who interact with each other five days a week, month after month, year after year. If someone smells, everyone knows it! Don't be that person! How can you tell if you *are* that person? Well, you might be the smelly one if others:

Recoil on sight.

Find a reason to cover their noses.

Offer you gum while you're talking.

Turn away as you approach.

Half-gag.

Or have this look plastered across their faces.

This is especially true in the service industry, where putting people at ease and not ruining their appetites is the name of the game. If you want to earn good tips, avoid body odor and bad breath. Smell like nothing in particular, and you'll be a winner!

A Successful Attitude

More than what you wear or how you smell, it's important to have the right attitude when you come to work each day. Be ready to roll up your sleeves and put your nose to the grindstone.

If you normally lead a glamorous lifestyle, don't let your social life intrude on your professional life. People are counting on you!

Sometimes this may mean slowing down a bit.

If you can't take your foot off the gas—if you find your lifestyle is undermining your productivity—seek help.

Most of all, when you arrive at work, you are setting the tone for your whole day. You may have deadlines, meetings, and responsibilities to juggle, but ease into your day with a calm demeanor and a confident smile.

Your coworkers will notice. If you arrive with a negative attitude, people will tend to avoid you for the rest of the day. Maybe that's what you want, but that's not the way to get it.

When You're Late

People are late to work all the time. It happens. And it is okay to be late every once in a while, but it can't happen every other day. This is what bosses call being "chronically late," and it does not look good on your performance review. However, whether this is your first time or your hundredth time, there are some things that you can do to at least improve the situation.

Just like homework, it doesn't do anyone any good to make up dramatic excuses. If you're late, you're late. It doesn't really matter why. Simply apologize and get right to work.

Everyone comes in late every once in a while. Everyone knows that sometimes the traffic really is bad on Highway 101 and you're not just making it up.

Even if you are, keep it simple. It's more convincing than some loud, involved story. If someone asks what happened, simply say:

No one can argue with a faulty alarm clock. And people will appreciate your coolness under pressure. That is a highly valued skill in the workplace.

WHEN CALLING IN SICK

Same song, different tune. If you're sick, you're sick. If you can't come in to work, simply call or email your boss and let him or her know. Say you're not feeling well, so you will be taking a sick day, and you're sorry for any inconvenience.

> I'm not feeling well, so I'm going to take a sick day. I'm sorry for any inconvenience.

It really is as simple as that. You don't need to be dramatic. This isn't acting class.

> I think I am dying . . . of a shark bite.

So long as your company is part of an industrialized nation, you will have sick days allotted to you. These days, many companies don't even waste time calling them "sick" days, since people get "sick" so often. It may be called "allotted time off," which you can use whenever and however you see fit.

Whatever the case, when you come in the next day, people will ask if you're feeling better and/or what was wrong. Maybe they care about you, and maybe they are just nosy. But you need to tell them something. So again, avoid the dramatics and keep it simple.

> I feel a lot better today, I just had an off day.

IN A MEETING

Meetings provide an opportunity for everyone to join together in discussing collaborative projects, work schedules, and common problems. Meetings are great time-saving devices. Imagine having to talk to each person individually. It would take forever.

Using the Time Well

Wasting time in meetings is a pet peeve of managers and coworkers alike. Don't be guilty of this offense! Meetings usually have an allotted amount of time, and then people need to get back to their desks. So, in meetings, don't let your mind wander; try to stay on track.

Avoid open-ended statements and general observations.

Make a real effort to contribute something of value. Do not talk just to prove how much you know.

If you're unsure, ask yourself the following questions:

Above all, a meeting shouldn't be a contest of wills for control of the discussion. A little listening goes a long way.

IN WORK CORRESPONDENCE

The internet and email have completely transformed the workplace (for more advice on dealing with the internet, see "On the Internet," page 171). It used to be that we sat at desks writing with quills and ink, then we tapped at IBM Selectric typewriters, and now we sit in front of our computers all day long. It's amazing how things change!

Email

As a form of communication at work, email deserves special mention here. Perhaps the most obvious thing about it is that we can "talk" to someone without getting up from our desk or shouting across the room. This is a revolution offices were long waiting for.

However, email comes with its own pitfalls and dangers. Emails can often seem less urgent than phone calls, for instance, and they can also lead to a more impersonal style of address. So the tone of our emails can often seem harsher or more curt than we intended.

Communicate politely, and make requests nicely; thank people for their time. Adding a few exclamation points or a smiley face is a great way to convey a friendly tone! Most important of all, don't hit send before reading your email. Make sure it says only what you want to say and nothing extra, and make sure you only send it to the people who need to see it. Even the friendliest email in the world won't be appreciated by those who aren't meant to receive it. They get enough email already!

IN THE BREAK ROOM

Most offices have a common room where all workers can eat lunch and "take a break" from their hectic jobs. Just like living with roommates, everyone has to take care of the break room together. So clean your area after using it; a little maintenance goes a long way.

The Microwave

When using the microwave, put a paper plate on top of your food to ensure it doesn't splatter all over the place. Then wipe out the microwave afterward. This is a workplace, not a science experiment.

IT'S ALIVE!

The Communal Refrigerator

The first rule of the break room is that other people's food is off-limits. No matter how much better it is than your soggy sandwich, don't eat other people's lunch from the fridge. This has been the cause of many workplace arguments.

Where is my GOUDA?!

If someone *does* steal your food, do not leave passive-aggressive notes. Remember: You are just trying to reach one person, but a note infuriates everybody.

If you find your food is being eaten, try using a lockable box. Or keep your lunch at your desk in a cooler pack or mini-refrigerator. The thief will then move on to easier pickings.

Loose Lips Sink Ships

Finally, while the break room is a place to relax, don't drop your guard completely. You never know who may be in the break room with you. Keep your conversation light. If you have a personal topic to share or too much anger to hold inside, take it outside of the building.

In the Bathroom

It's important to treat your work bathroom in the same way that you would treat your home bathroom. Which basically means you need to clean up after yourself! It's only respectful to those using the restroom after you.

Lift the Seat, Gentlemen

One of the most frustrating things for bathroom users is finding pee on the seat. Yuck!

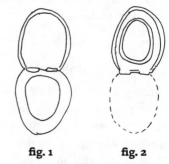

fig. 1   fig. 2

You may think that you have great aim, but this is not target practice. Save that for outside. At work, take the extra time to lift both the lid and the seat. Then, if you forget or your aim isn't all that it once was, simply wipe off any wayward drops.

Wipe the Seat, Ladies

Now we will address the ladies' room! Ladies, you know there's nothing worse than finding a peed-on seat. But here's a news flash: It's not just the boys who are the culprits. Many ladies are grossed out by public bathrooms and prefer to hover over the seat while peeing. The less contact with the seat, they think, the better. However, more distance means more splashing. And where does all that splashing urine land? On the seat.

Be polite and keep it tidy, ladies! Take the time to wipe it down afterwards!

Or, use a seat cover.

And if seat covers are not in supply, you can make your own out of toilet paper! DIY sanitation!

fig. 1   **fig. 2**

The Stall Is Not an Office

When people say they need to go "take care of some business," they don't mean actual business! So get in and get out. Don't stand in front of the stalls chatting with your friends, tweeting updates on your cell phone. This can make other people feel uncomfortable.

Always Wash Your Hands

When you're at work, that sign means you!

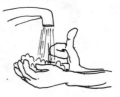

When You Hate the Boss

A good boss is hard to find. And even the best bosses can become tiring after enough time. In fact, your relationship with your boss might seem a lot more like a friend, sibling, or even a parent.

If you are having trouble with your boss, try to keep a few things in mind. First, try to understand the boss's perspective. They have a lot riding on their shoulders: meetings to deal with, a team to run, bottom lines to watch, and people's feelings to keep from stomping all over.

Receiving Criticism

Most bosses would love it if all they had to do was praise their workers. But unfortunately, part of a boss's job is to let employees know when they are doing something wrong or not working to their full potential. When this happens, it's important to handle such feedback in a professional way.

Listen to what your boss is telling you without becoming defensive or going on the attack. No matter how unfair the criticism might be, it is not a good idea to lose your temper. Remain calm and collected. When your boss is finished, thank her for caring so much about you and your work.

Later on, if you disagree with your boss's criticism or you feel she may have confused you with another worker, approach her in a nonconfrontational manner and ask her if you could chat for a minute.

Let her know, in a professional manner, how you feel.

By accepting criticism and working together with your boss to solve the problem, you can both create a better, more efficient workplace.

When You Are the Boss

If you have worked your way to the top of the ladder, congratulations are in order. Here are some helpful tips to ensure that your time in charge runs smoothly. First, enjoy the view while it lasts.

Lunch is for wimps.

Building Team Spirit

As the boss, you have a team of people looking to you for leadership. So lead! Give them direction and work to do.

That dog will need banners! American flags! And a baby! Who has a baby that the dog can kiss at the next debate?

Hey, I just noticed the poll numbers were a little off. Let's go over the numbers during lunch!

But don't be tyrannical about it. People respond better when they are confident and happy in their work. If a problem arises, pull the relevant people aside and talk to them in private. This will lessen their embarrassment in front of the rest of the team.

Then, present the problem as you see it, express what you expect from your team, and suggest ways you can work together to fix things. It is a privilege to have people work for you. Never take that for granted. Remember: You may be the boss, but you're not a dictator!

You can still be a tough boss, and you can push people to work their hardest, just make sure that you never treat people disrespectfully. After all, they're the ones doing most of the work. Treat your employees fairly, and everyone profits!

Wielding Power

As a boss, you have a lot of power. In some positions, you may find your power to effect change extends beyond the board-room and into society itself. Lots of people—and even other companies—may listen closely to what you say and do.

Perhaps you've found a loophole in government regulations—
one that can make those able to exploit it very rich.

Just make sure you always consider the larger ramifications
of your actions.

When Working from Home

Whether we're talking about flex time, work from home, or part-time hours, today's evolving employment policies have many benefits. At home, workers can meet deadlines, respond to emails, and check in on projects in pajamas or stretch pants!

When Using a Coffee Shop as Your Office

With a Wi-Fi connection or an internet link, you can work from almost anywhere: a park, a train, the doctor's office, or the beach. A coffee shop, for instance, often offers a constant supply of Wi-Fi. Plus, it provides you with a change of scenery.

Just remember: A coffee shop is also a business and someone else's workplace. Be courteous and respectful. And be sure to tip the staff.

Treat servers like your coworkers and the coffee shop owner like your landlord—one who charges really cheap rent.

If business is slow, then using an entire table all day is usually no problem. Just keep smiling and ordering another cup of joe. However, if the coffee shop gets crowded, share your table with others, or take a much-needed break. Your fellow work-at-homers will appreciate it!

The coffee shop will appreciate it, too. If your presence drives customers away and the coffee shop loses money, then it might go out of business. Then where will everyone go to work at "home"? Do your part. After all, "It takes a village!"

At Office Parties

When your work day is done, try to enjoy some time out with a few coworkers. This can be a great way to bond and learn more about them. The same is true for any parties your office hosts. Take the opportunities that birthdays and other office parties provide to talk about things other than work or to pass along praise you just didn't get a chance to share during your busy day.

Keep the conversation fun and light! Talk about sports, funny viral videos, music, or news of the world. Avoid getting too personal or passing judgment on what people do in their off-hours. People are bummed out enough during work. They don't want to be bummed out after work, too!

Behave Responsibly

If you go out after work with your team, it's fine to relax. That's the whole point. But don't get *too* relaxed. Let your hair down, just not all the way. Remember: You'll be seeing all these people again tomorrow!

So pay attention to what you drink—and order thoughtfully.

If anything, you want to stay behind the curve on the party's enthusiasm. Find your happy place and maintain it.

The main reason for this is so that your mouth doesn't become disconnected from your brain. The last thing you want is to replace your eyeglasses with sarsaparilla goggles and to start voicing inappropriate remarks about someone you work with.

These are your coworkers, not your close friends. Avoid off-color remarks, no matter how funny you may think they are. Remain professional and treat everyone with respect.

The Next Day

Okay, it happens. Everyone makes a faux pas at one time or another. If you feel you have behaved inappropriately or spoken out of turn, take a moment to review the situation. Perhaps you made fun of your boss?

Or maybe you made advances toward a coworker?

Or maybe you're just not sure what you did. Well, if it's juicy, you can bet other people in your office won't have forgotten what happened.

Then she ran around with the toupee in her hand pretending it was a flying cat!

By the next day, there's nothing you can do about it. The story will get around. Don't be surprised if it even gets a little exaggerated.

She threw the toupee in the punch. Then drank the ENTIRE BOWL!

I'm sorry I stole your toupee and played "monkey in the middle" with it!

In that case, apologize to any inadvertent victims of your behavior.

So the lesson is: Don't steal people's hair. I guess I learned the hard way.

Then, remember that most people do something that they are embarrassed about at one point or another. Take your own embarrassment in stride.

IN AN OFFICE ROMANCE

If you spend a lot of time at work, you might meet someone you're interested in. While it's okay to mix business with pleasure, it's not prudent to enjoy that pleasure during business hours. From nine to five, you have a job to do, so focus on doing it.

Before You Dive In

Dating someone else is never a simple proposition, and dating someone you're working with increases the complication factor significantly. So before you get involved with a coworker, take a moment to reflect.

Avoiding the Appearance of Impropriety

If you do decide that you're ready to instigate an office romance, be aware that your relationship is likely to draw some attention. In fact, some people may wonder if the motives on both sides are entirely pure. This is another important question to ask yourself before diving in: Are you likely to receive preferential treatment as a result of this relationship? If your work responsibilities shift as your relationship changes, that's a problem. And if you find yourself in that situation, you're likely to feel some tension from your coworkers as well.

But if everything is aboveboard and everyone's mature enough to give this relationship a shot, you should still make an extra effort to keep your relationship to yourself. Don't share the details of your romantic life with the whole office. If you have a fight, or break up, act as if nothing has changed.

Before   **After**

DURING PERFORMANCE REVIEWS

Performance reviews are stressful. They can also be frustrating, especially if you feel you are not being compensated fairly for your work. Perhaps you suspect that your boss has some unspoken bias—be it gender or racial, or that of a jilted lover—and that he or she is deliberately holding you back. Nevertheless, it is not a good strategy to cry or lose your temper during a performance review.

Like umpires in baseball, bosses aren't likely to change their call just because you are crying or yelling at them. In fact, these are forms of emotional manipulation and display poor judgment. Remain professional and outline your disagreements in a respectful way. Understand they may not have control in the situation, and ask them what you can do to improve your chances of success in the future.

Asking for a Raise

Many employees take the opportunity of a performance review to ask for a raise. If that's your plan, take care to get your ducks in a row first, and make sure you're prepared to state your case.

Have you been working hard and achieving deadlines?

Have you been exceeding goals and performing duties beyond your job description?

Have you been putting in more hours than are required?

If so, then you are on the fast track to success! In addition, you have good grounds to ask for a raise. When the moment is right, politely state your case.

Most companies are happy to reward employees who work hard. Of course, those rewards may vary. If a clap on the back or a holiday cheese log doesn't fit your expectations, be honest about how you feel and present solid evidence that your employer's compensation doesn't meet industry standards. Show examples and present charts for why you deserve a higher income. At the very least, let your boss know that you're disappointed.

When Leaving a Job

Nothing lasts forever, and that includes employment. Perhaps you found a better job, or you're moving away, or you're going back to school to be retrained in a profession that pays a living wage. Whatever the case, here's some advice for when it's time to seek new horizons.

Giving Notice

If you're leaving your job, give your boss a reasonable amount of notice. Two weeks is considered standard, but of course, it depends. Two weeks gives the company at least a reasonable amount of time to fill your position with a minimum of upheaval.

Be nice about it. They're the ones who have to stay behind, after all. Thank your boss and coworkers for the opportunity to learn and grow with them.

When You're Fired

If you've been fired, you might feel angry. In fact, you might want to leave in a dramatic fashion.

However, it's unwise to burn your bridges. You never know what the future may bring. You might need your boss's recommendation. You may even want your old job back.

Try leaving on a good note. No matter how good or bad your time has been, you've certainly learned something.

When You're Unemployed

You may consider unemployment terrifying, or perhaps a blessed relief, but being without a job doesn't mean there isn't work to do. You have to apply for unemployment benefits, first of all, and of course, you have to find a new position. So keep your head up and make do with the money you saved when you were employed. That rainy day you were waiting for? It's here!

No rainy day fund? Well, don't get mad at your friends just because they're still having fun.

Instead, suggest something you all can do together that costs little or no money.

CHAPTER 5
At Play

AT A PARTY

Parties are an enjoyable time for all young ladies and gentlemen. You get a chance to make new friends, create stronger bonds with old friends, and maybe even meet someone special. Parties are fun and exciting!

Getting Ready

Getting ready for a party can some-times be the best part. First there is the anticipation of mingling with your peers and taking a refreshing break from studying and housework. Who will be there, and what will they wear? Speaking of clothes, picking  out your own can be super fun. Is the party fancy or casual? Remember, not every social gathering requires you to dress up.

When You Arrive

Always say hello to the host of the party and thank her for your invitation. She went out of her way to get all those lovely people together. Show your appreciation by bring-ing a gift—something that everyone at the party can partake in. If the place is decorated, comment on how lovely  it looks. If that's not possible, mention how much you like the music. If that is also difficult, ask where the bathroom is.

Flirting

Oh, look! There is that girl from English class that you've been dreaming about. She seems to be between conversations and you'd like to approach her. This is the moment you've been waiting for all night, and you don't want to blow it. What should you do?

First, don't overlook the simplest approach. Just say hello and introduce yourself.

If you already know each other, break the ice with an observation about the party or inquire about a common school or work project. Discussing the music that's playing is also a great conversation starter.

If you find the prospect of striking up a conversation with someone you're physically attracted to absolutely terrifying, then give yourself a pep talk first (for more advice on starting a conversation with a potential mate, see "In Conversation," page 28).

All the same cautions and strategies apply. One big difference is that when you are flirting, it's okay to convey that you're keen on someone. That's the whole idea! Just be careful to avoid comments that are offensive or invasive. People like to feel pretty or handsome, but they tend to be less fond of being treated like a prime cut of beef.

Just act casual and natural. Be yourself. Don't come on hard with a prefabricated pick-up line.

You can compliment someone's grooming and appearance without sounding like a total dick.

Such comments are flattering, and they let people know you think they are special. Once the ball is rolling, ask about their opinions, interests, likes and dislikes—as if you were interested in them in all their uniqueness. After all, that's how you want them to treat you!

Turn Off Social Media Devices

At a party, the best advice is to turn off ALL social media devices. Why do you need them, anyway? You're at a party! If by mistake you have one sugary beverage too many, you will be broadcasting your blunders live. In the morning, even *you* will not understand why you retweeted the same movie quote twenty-seven times. Or why you used so many extra vowels and punctuation.

Whaaa??! OMG, no wayyyyyy!

You may find yourself tempted to get into a fight over text with a friend or message your ex. Or you might spend the whole party watching YouTube videos of dogs on a swing. To be safe, just turn it all off.

Changing the Music

Good music is essential to any successful party. Just remember: Everyone has different tastes. If you feel an intense desire to change the music, be careful.

After all, you don't want to accidentally insult the host's taste!

Ugh, this band is old news.

Instead, ask politely first.

If the host says yes, wait for the current song to finish playing. Do not stop a song abruptly in the middle. Even if the song is terrible, wait it out.

This will keep the flow of the party going. When the song is finished, cue up the music you prefer and press play.

Once you've had a chance to DJ for a while, allow someone else to step in. Who knows, that person might play something you like. Above all, keep it light! Parties are meant to be fun!

One note about musical irony: If there is music you like only because it was Top 40s when you were ten, make sure everyone is in on the joke. Otherwise, someone's head might explode.

Finally, if the host locks her computer or has created a special playlist for the party, do not press her to change the music. It's her party. She can do what she wants to.

Beverages

Parties thrive on beverages. Talking is thirsty work! But follow the laws in your area, and enjoy your sugary beverages in moderation.

There's always the danger that too much liquid inspiration— too much of a sugar high, so to speak—could lead to some mistakes. And you don't want to wind up with clouded judgment. You may think you're reciting Shakespeare when in reality you're saying utter nonsense.

Instead, know your limits, and surround yourself with people you trust. If you do get carried away, you want your friends to look out for you and not draw a moustache on your face.

You're Out of Control

A lot of dickish things can happen when parties get too wild. Make sure you have friends you can trust and that they have your best interests at heart.

If you are buzzing on sugar or if someone spiked the punch, DO NOT DRIVE. Use a designated driver, call a taxi, or ask someone to come get you.

If the only way you can get home is to drive yourself, then don't go home. Stay where you are and sleep it off. Seriously.

Secondly, other people can be dicks and take advantage of someone who has had too much punch. Be sure to surround yourself with people you trust! If people are being dicks and trying to take advantage of you, it's okay to give them hell.

Someone Else Is Drunk

If other people drink too much of that punch, don't be a dick. Help them out. Make sure they don't embarrass themselves or hurt themselves. First, take their keys.

Second, if you can drive them home safely, do so. Otherwise, help them call a friend or a car service.

Treat others the way you would like to be treated if you were in the same predicament. Give them water while they wait for their ride.

Leaving the Party

When you decide to leave, always thank your host. Tell him or her you had a lovely time. If you didn't, mention how much you loved the music.

Finally, if you brought a gift and see that it is unfinished or unopened, DO NOT take it with you. This may be tempting, as you slaved all day making that meatloaf. However, just think of it as payment for the host having to clean up the entire mess from the party.

AT A RESTAURANT

Everybody likes going out to a nice restaurant for a good meal. While it seems like this should be simple, there are a lot of ways it can go wrong. Here's what you need to know to do things right.

Respect Your Server

Waiters are not your servants. They are just doing their job, which is to take your order and serve your food. Maybe they are young and it's their first job, or maybe it's the best they can do in a tough economy, or maybe they just love the job, but whatever the case, you should absolutely not be condescending.

I'm going to order a long list of things and not look at you once.

If you want good service, be polite to the waitstaff. Treat them with respect and show appreciation for their help.

I would like a ham sandwich. Thank you for your help!

Just because waiters take your order and bring you your food, it doesn't mean they're in dire need of your advice.

What you have to do is start a blog! Just start a blog! I read an article in the *New York Times* about a mom in Texas who did that, and now she has a book deal.

So . . . what are you waiting for?

You have no idea what they are doing with their lives. Treat them with respect, and stay out of it.

Getting Your Waiter's Attention

The best way to get your waiter's attention, especially when the restaurant is busy, is to lift your hand and say, "Excuse me," when your server walks by.

Try not to whistle.

Or snap.

And no matter how loud it is, it is important not to yell. Your server can see and hear you just fine.

Ordering Your Food

The reason restaurants print a menu is to let you know what food they serve. Use it. It's okay to request a small change to a dish. Just tell your server clearly what you want.

Accommodating special requests takes more work than you might think. Typically, the kitchen preps the food before the dinner shift. The meatballs are already made; the paninis are stacked and ready to be pressed. The kitchen cannot unmake a soup to take out the carrots. While some changes are possible, if a restaurant's menu has nothing on it that you like, the best approach is to find a new restaurant.

Allergies and Dietary Restrictions

If you have any allergies, let your server know before ordering. The server will have a better sense of what ingredients each menu item contains, and he or she can notify the kitchen.

In general, it is considered very rude to bring in food from another restaurant.

However, if you are bringing food from home for a specific purpose—for a birthday, say, or to accommodate an allergy—that is often allowed. Explain what you are doing, and tip your server a little extra to compensate for the lower bill and extra work.

Dealing with Unruly Diners

When dining out, you may occasionally find your dining experience interrupted by other patrons who are behaving in a manner that is less than civilized.

At those moments, it's important to remember that not all patrons are equally culpable.

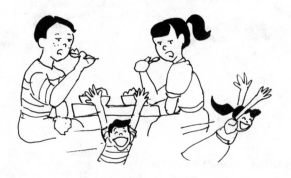

Maybe they had a long day.

Maybe they haven't had enough long days.

But even if they have *no* good excuse as far as you can see—even if they *are* acting like dicks—that's no reason to return the favor.

The restaurant is a common space. If someone is not respecting that common space, let the waiter know so that he can either handle it himself or else alert the management.

Speaking to someone who actually works there—rather than addressing the problem yourself—also provides a filter, which can help situations from rapidly deteriorating.

A Note on Children

Think of the situation from a kid's perspective: Restaurants are BORING. Waiting for food is boring. There are a bunch of grown-ups there, talking about grown-up stuff, drinking grown-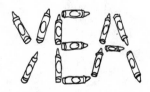up drinks, and everyone is wearing boring grown-up clothes. So if you happen to be in the company of very small children, keep their brains occupied. Offer crayons and coloring books, or just some plain paper! Let them draw away while you talk.

Maybe they have a favorite handheld game. Let them play with that with the sound off.

Encourage them stay in their seats.

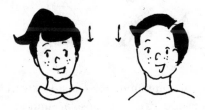

And remind them to say please and thank you.

In the case where a child in your party has a temper tantrum in a restaurant, you may have to call dinner quits for the night. Unfortunately, it is not a good idea to tough it out, because you will be making those around you tough it out as well.

As the older, wiser companion, be considerate of how the children's actions are affecting those around you.

Making Complaints

Lots of people have off days, and sometimes the food or the service is not ideal. The best way to handle it is calmly. Don't take a mistake personally. Explain what you're unhappy about. Most of the time, the staff will try to make it up to you, particularly if you're being nice and kind about it.

If you would like to return your food, it's best to do it right away. Do not wait to complain until your plate is almost empty. Otherwise, the staff may get the impression that you're trying to get a free meal.

Avoid yelling or talking down to your server about the food.

You attract more bees with honey than with vinegar. A pleasant attitude might attract a free dessert, whereas a bad one will only net you bad memories.

Tipping

After a meal, be sure to tip your waiter. Even if you have some complaints, leave something. Most of a server's earnings come from tips, and servers have to tip out the rest of the service staff: the bussers, food runners, bartenders, and hosts. If you have good service and tip well, your server will remember you and be happy to see you next time. Here's a quick guide for standard tips:

10%: Delivery

10%: Poor Service

15%: Moderate Service

18–20%: Good to Great Service

20–25%: Amazing Service!

25% and up: If a team of masters from *Top Chef* kills, cooks, and serves all of your food (in diamond-studded roller skates).

Out on the Town

Sometimes it's fun to go out even when you don't have a party to attend. After all, cafes, juice bars, and the local drugstore have everything that parties have—fizzy drinks, tasty snacks, and great music—but none of the hassle. (That is, as long as everyone is able to keep from behaving like a dick. Speaking of which . . . !)

Ordering a Drink

Unless it's 10 a.m. on Monday morning, most food and drink establishments are busy places. Help yourself out—and do your local soda jerk a favor at the same time—by deciding what you'd like to drink before you belly up to the bar. If you need time to think, that's okay, just step aside and allow the other patrons to order ahead of you.

When it's busy, there's nothing worse than people elbowing their way up to the rail and then just standing there thinking when the soda jerk is ready to take their order.

Uhhhhhhhhh.

Soda jerks don't have time for that. They have their hands full trying to keep a roomful of people happy.

I would like something savory, my good man—and with gin!

If it's not busy, that's the perfect time to ask the person behind the counter what he'd recommend. He may inquire about your palate: Do you like sweet, savory, or bitter? Specify the type of beverage you're in the mood for, and—who knows!—you might wind up with something really special.

When it comes to juices, it's important again to be specific. Because there are a number of subtle flavor differences to consider.

I would like a dry red grape drink, from the Loire Valley. What would you recommend?

Buybacks

Here's a tip: If you've been sipping on soda all night long and tipping after each round—as you should!—the soda jerk may give you a "buyback." This is his special way of saying thank you. Typically, this only happens for regulars, or if you have bought three or more drinks, and/or if you seem like a nice

polite person. The first rule of
thumb with a buyback is not to
expect it.

It doesn't matter how cutely or
coyly you say it. You just sound
like a mooch.

Waiters and soda jerks enjoy being generous when they can,
but they get annoyed when people act entitled. Besides, some
soda shop managers don't even allow buybacks. So, if you are
bestowed with one of these lovely little sweet treats, smile, say
thank you, and then consider dropping a couple extra bucks in
the tip jar. This is karma in action.

Falling for the Soda Jerk

Soda jerks—like
all bartenders—are
great listeners, and
sometimes you can't
help but have a crush
on that cute boy
who's making all your

malteds! If you start having tender feelings for your server,
know that you are not alone. Also, remember that he is at
work, and he may not be on the same kind of sugar high that
you're on.

So if you really do like your local soda jerk, return in the light of day and flirt with him before you've had four spritzers too many. It's a sign of respect as well as a good reality check. Besides, think of it from the soda jerk's perspective: Would you want to be stuck in a tiny space and leered at like a zoo animal all night?

Becoming Unreasonable

There are all kinds of over-imbibers. Sugar slobs, ice cream dreamers, soda soakers, and so on. But the one thing they all have in common, when they've had too much of their beverage of choice, is an absurd confidence in their own opinion. They're so hopped up on sugar and soda water that nothing anyone else can say will ever change their minds. This is an unfortunate situation.

If you recognize that you have become unreasonable, go home. Stop yourself before you get into a fight, whether verbal or physical. Your friends aren't trying to ruin your night by telling you to calm down. They are trying to keep themselves from getting tossed out of the drugstore right along with you. So if you get to a point where everyone seems to have turned against you, call it a night.

When Running Errands

Errands are more like work than play, but they're a real necessity. After all, it's hard to play without food, furniture, and clean clothes.

At the Grocery Store

How you approach grocery shopping makes all the difference. If you go to the store without any idea of what you already have or what you want, you are likely to stand around in confusion, blocking the aisles. This will not be appreciated by fellow shoppers.

So, before going to the store, look in your pantry and your fridge and make a list of what you need. A thorough list can make all the difference. Not only that, it will save you from returning home and realizing you forgot something essential.

One of the great joys of grocery shopping is free samples! You get to try out new things and perhaps even turn it into an impromptu free meal. However, be polite. Take only one sample at a time. Then shop for a while before returning for more. Act curious and intrigued, not hungry. Don't just grab as many pigs in a blanket as you can.

If you need help finding something or getting something down
from a high shelf, look for someone to help you. Don't stand in the
aisle shouting for help.

Finally, when your cart is full, and
you've checked off everything
on your list, it's time to check out.
Even if all the cashiers are busy,
never cut in line. That may be the
worst sin of grocery store etiquette.
If you are unsure if someone is in
line, ask them first.

Sometimes, a new register will
open. Be polite and ask the person
ahead of you if he or she would like
to take it. Do not beeline for the
open checkout.

At a Swedish Furniture Store

Swedish furniture stores are like
a dream come true. They sell
stylish, cheap furniture that's
always in stock and easy to put
together. You don't even need
to speak Swedish! However, be
warned: These stores are set up
like a maze, and it can be hard to
find your way out.

Since furniture is heavy, you will
be tempted to ask someone to come along with you. You will
need an extra set of hands. But a word to the wise: Go on your

own first and figure out everything you want. It is impossible to
breeze in and out. Your shopping
companion will appreciate your
consideration, and it also doesn't
hurt to offer a token of your grati-
tude while you're in the store.

We can get ice
cream and horse-meat
meatballs after this!
On me!

Also, don't come if you are feeling under the
weather. The bold florescent lights, recycled
air, and aimless crowds pushing oversized
purchases are like a sharp poke in the eye.
You will want to lie down in a bedroom display. No one wants to see that.

At the Laundromat

At some point, pretty much everyone
has to do without a washer and dryer
at home. But don't be intimated! Sur-
viving the laundromat is easy, so long
as you can get there before everybody
else. Laundromats tend to be busiest
during weeknights and on the weekend, so if that's the only time you have
available, you should just be aware
that you'll probably have to wait a
little bit. If you go in with reasonable
expectations, it will be easier to cope

with a few delays. Just decide which machine you'd like to use,
and put your bag on top of it or your cart of clothes in front of
it. That way other people will know that you're next in line for
that machine.

If a load of clothes is finished, but the owner is nowhere to be seen, ask the attendant to remove them for you. It's just not a good idea to remove other people's clothes yourself.

And if you do expect delays, bring something to occupy yourself, such as a book or a smartphone. If you decide to leave between loads, don't lose track of the time, or you may return to find all your clothes in wet piles.

CHAPTER 6

In Transit

On Trains and Buses

Public transportation is cheap, energy efficient, and (when it's at its best) convenient, too. But it's also, without a doubt, "mass transit." And that can present some real problems. Sometimes it can feel as crowded as a sardine can. In these moments, smile and try not to dwell on how uncomfortable you are. After all, you're not the only one!

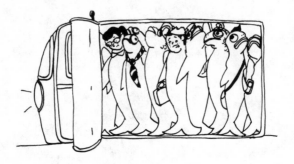

Before Your Ride Arrives

When a train or bus arrives, everyone is eager to get on quickly and find a seat. But that's just the thing: Everyone is in the same boat! (So to speak.) So be considerate, pay attention, and follow the rules—whether they're written down or not.

The first rule of public transportation is: Don't block the exits.

Let other people exit first. When the exits have cleared, go with the flow.

Sitting

There's nothing better than finding an open seat on a train or bus. A seat allows you to rest your tired feet. However, if you find a seat for yourself, make sure that you're not monopolizing the seats of others with your legs, bags, or other luggage. Be conscientious.

Try to find a way to get comfort-able, but don't spread your legs as if you were on your couch at home.

Avoid crossing your legs as well, which does nothing but take up more space.

Finally, if you are seated, and you see someone who is pregnant, elderly, injured, or otherwise in more need of a seat than you are yourself, get up and offer that person your seat.

Talking on the Phone

On a bus or a train, silence is golden. It's best to text while traveling with others, but if you do need to talk on the phone, try and keep your voice down and the time of the conversation as a whole to a minimum. Other riders don't want to spend their whole ride listening to your conversation!

Yeah, I've like been killing it in corn lately.

Listening to Music

Listening to music on public transportation is a great idea. It's always fun to put together your own personal commuter mix.

Just make sure to wear a pair of nifty headphones.

Then, select an appropriate volume level. Make sure it's not *too* loud.

The same goes for singing. Public transportation is not a talent competition. If you must sing, hold out your hat so people will think you're busking. They still won't like it, but they might give you money so you'll move along.

Or, better yet, save it for recording at home!

On Airplanes

Transportation by train, plane, and automobile all require the same attention to basic human decency, but plane travel has a few extra wrinkles in it that need some extra attention.

Reclining Seats

One of the luxuries of plane travel is the ability to recline your seat. Nothing could be more relaxing!

Unfortunately, airplane designers forgot to consider the people sitting behind each seat. Just because you can recline all the way, it doesn't mean you should. And if you do really crave those few extra degrees, politely ask the person behind you if he wouldn't mind before you intrude on his space.

After all, wouldn't you appreciate the same courtesy?

Armrests

Airplane armrests are a delight, but there are never enough.

If a row has three seats, it holds three people, who possess a total of six arms. But there are only four armrests! There will always be two left over.

Often, the two people seated on the outside seats will take two armrests each, leaving the middle person with none—and two very tired arms.

The person in the middle is already in a tough spot. She can't look out the window. She doesn't have access to the aisle. And now this. At some point or another, we will all be that monkey in the middle. So stand up for the middle person! If you are on the outside, make do with one armrest, and leave the two in the middle for the person in the middle. Then everyone gets something! (Or, at the very least, rotate.)

Taking Off Your Shoes

Another joy of flying is the ability to remove your shoes! On long flights, it may even be necessary. But like always, ensure that your comfort doesn't intrude on the people around you.

Before flying, put on clean socks. Give your travel shoes the sniff test. If they don't pass, choose another pair. If all you own is one cruddy pair of stinky shoes, buy deodorant-scented insoles. Then enjoy your flight!

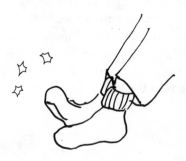

In Taxis

In a taxi, you have considerably more privacy than you do in other modes of public transportation. But remember: The driver is there, too! Always treat the driver with respect. Be polite when giving directions and stating your destination. Though taxi drivers make a living picking people up, they have every right to kick you out if you're disrespectful.

Respect the taxi*cab* as well. The cab is often the driver's own personal property, and other people will be riding in it after you. If you eat or open purchases in the cab, do not leave trash behind. Sure, you can talk with friends or on your phone, but still, use your inside voice so as not to distract the driver.

If they've been doing it for long enough, cab drivers have basically seen it all. But do yourself a favor and don't provide them with any additional fodder for their "bad passenger" stories. They don't need any new material.

In Automobiles

When it comes to privacy in transit, you can't beat your own car. Cars come with their own fair share of troubles and trials, but there are few things better than an open road and a full tank of gas (or a full charge on your electric vehicle). Here's what you can do to keep things smooth while on the road yourself.

Texting

The only thing you should do while driving is drive. Texting while driving is extremely, extremely dangerous. Anything that forces you to take your eyes off the road should be avoided at all costs.

 If you're stopped at a red light, you might think, "Okay, now I can shoot out a text real quick." But guess what? The light will turn green even quicker. Save it for later.

Road Rage

Anyone can drive. Absolutely anyone. This means putting up with a wide range of interpersonal skills, attention levels, and basic competence behind the wheel. Some days, the behavior of other drivers may make you angry.

Just remember, yelling and screaming does not solve anything, and it deteriorates your own driving skills. If you find that you cannot calm down, pull over and take a breath. Otherwise, anything can happen.

Horn Use

Your car's horn is a warning device to alert other vehicles to the possibility of a collision or other danger. Do not use your horn unless absolutely necessary. The sound is meant to be jarring, so everyone within earshot will snap to attention. Using horns in other situations—such as expressing your annoyance or while playing the drums—will not be appreciated by others. So cool it.

ON BICYCLES AND TRICYCLES

Bike commuting is becoming increasingly popular, as it promotes an active lifestyle and decreases pollution. It's fun, free, and excellent exercise. Hurray for bikes!

Basic Safety

Like any mode of transportation, however, cycling has its perils. If you're not careful, it can result in injury or even death. So follow these safe-riding tips!

First, wear a helmet. If you are an adult, ride on the road, which hopefully will have a designated bike lane just for you. If it doesn't, write your elected representative and ask for one! Avoid riding on the sidewalk. You will take up too much room and could hurt a pedestrian!

Try to avoid weaving in and out of traffic. While bikes are nimble and easy to maneuver, cars are not.

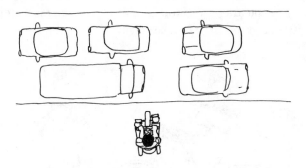

When children are biking, it's a different story. The road is too dangerous, and cars can't see them. So, kids, bike on the sidewalk! Save racing for the park, and keep to your right.

Ride with Traffic

When you ride your bike with traffic, you flow more easily with the cars around you. Also, it is safer for pedestrians! When crossing a street, a pedestrian will first look in the direction that cars are coming from.

Spare them a surprise and bike with traffic.

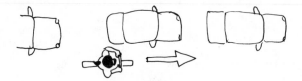

Follow Traffic Signals

Bicycles must follow the rules of the road, just like cars. In fact, though you might be riding a bike to avoid traffic, when you are on the road you are part of traffic. This means you must stop when there is a stop sign or a stoplight.

It also means you must yield to pedestrians at crosswalks.

Headphones

Don't ride your bike your with headphones on. This makes it difficult to hear cars and pedestrians. On a bicycle, this is an unsafe position to be in.

While Walking

So you may think, "I learned to walk when I was one. If there's one thing I know how to do, it's walk. I don't need some dumb book's advice!"

Wrong! There is walking, and then there is walking politely and with consideration for everyone around you. These are not the same thing!

Keep to the Right

The first rule of thumb is to walk like you're driving a car: Keep to the right, pass on the left.

Walking in the middle of the sidewalk makes it difficult for people to get around you on either side!

By doing this, you force others to go out of their way to accommodate you. Is that thoughtful or nice? No! So keep to the right.

Use Your Words

Whether you walk slow or fast, in a straight line or a meandering path, at some point you will need to get around someone else. When this happens, be polite. A simple "excuse me" usually does the trick.

Excuse me!

Do not get huffy. If the person does not hear you, politely tap her on the shoulder to get her attention.

As a rule, you should always keep your hands to yourself, but in this case, a polite tap on someone's shoulder is okay and even called for. However, do not jab, poke, punch, or grab the other person. Nor should you touch anything but the shoulder or upper arm. Certainly, do not push people out of the way.

If someone does not hear you, do not get his or her attention by yelling.

Just say, "Excuse me," tap the person's shoulder, and get on with your day.

Turning Blind Corners

Pay extra attention when walking on a city sidewalk. Tall buildings can block your view when you come to intersections or corners. If you aren't careful, you could collide with someone else.

So when you reach a corner, stop and look. If someone else is coming from the other direction at the same time, allow that person to pass, then go yourself.

Sightseeing

Maybe you are new to town or on vacation. Maybe you don't know where you're going or what you're doing. Whatever the reason, avoid meandering slowly and then abruptly stopping or walking while reading a foldout map or city guide. This can cause you to bump into others or cause others to bump into you.

If you really are sightseeing, step to the side and keep the walkway as clear as possible.

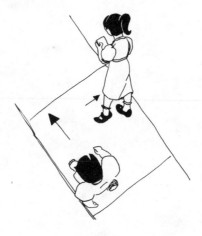

CHAPTER 7
On the Internet

WARNING: THE INTERNET IS FOREVER

We are living in a time when the whole world is literally at our fingertips. You'd think that would solve all our problems: No more misunderstandings, no more ignorance, no more bashing others without the facts! In short, no more dickishness! Unfortunately, no.

An Appropriate Level of Caution

The technology may have changed, but human nature hasn't. Like every modern convenience, the internet can be both a blessing and a curse. For instance, consider the fact that everything on the internet, for all intents and purposes, lives forever. Whatever you post on a blog or send to someone else never really completely disappears. It's like finding your embarrassing teenage journals in the basement, but unlike paper journals, you can't burn them, and everyone can read them.

When you post something on the internet, you have no control over it. Anyone can copy, repost, or link to it. Your privacy settings might help a little, but they are a false comfort. You have no control over people who might take a screenshot of your spelling and grammar errors and post them for strangers to see and comment on.

This may not seem like a big deal right now. Those photos of your "youthful indiscretions" can make for big laughs. You are just keeping it real. Who cares?

Your future employers, that's who. If you want to become a teacher or a child-care provider, do you really want the children you're helping and their parents to see this part of you?

Before you post, text, or tweet, take an extra second to consider what you are putting online. Your future self will appreciate it.

WHEN COMMENTING

One great thing about the internet is that anyone with an opinion can share. This is informative and helpful. We can tell people—even strang-  ers in foreign countries—what a great job they've done or how much we like what they've written, and we can also point out facts or perspectives they may have overlooked. Everyone appreciates honest praise and constructive criticism.

Then again, in every group of people, there are a few stinkers who try to ruin things for everyone. And when that group of people is made up of everyone on the internet, that's a lot of stinkers!

Appropriately Addressing the Topic

To avoid being a dick online, keep the following tips in mind. Make sure you're thoughtfully adding to the conversation, not pointing out a trivial mistake.

Avoid pointless statements that implicitly criticize others.

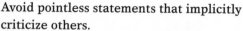

And remember that the world is a diverse place with many points of view. Just because people share their points of view doesn't mean that they don't understand your point of view or think it's invalid. Approach others and the internet with an open mind; you might learn something! Even if you don't, consider whether your comment addresses the topic at hand or is just venting frustration over the fact that not everyone is like you.

It never hurts to read other people's comments before posting your own. Perhaps others have made the same points already, or a comment thread has run off the rails and forgotten the original topic completely. Don't get sucked into these vortexes!

Reading the Entire Article

One rule of thumb: Always read the entire article before commenting. If you only read the headline or the first sentence, you don't know what the story or article is really about. The writer may have many nuanced points to make that address your concerns.

If you don't have time to read an entire article, don't comment on it.

Reading Is Private, Writing Is Public

When surfing the internet or texting with friends, it's easy to assume that what we are doing is private. We are in our own home, often alone, and perhaps communicating directly with only one person.

However, anything written or posted online—any comment, text, tweet, or photo—is public. In theory, anyone can see it. Even if you try to be anonymous, it's

very easy to find out who wrote what. In other words, a private reaction we have at home becomes public the moment we share it online. So, if you read something that makes you angry, take a breath and make sure you aren't about to act like a dick.

Profanity, Slagging, and Trolling

The internet creates a mask of privacy and anonymity. This can sometimes lead us to say and act online in ways we wouldn't if we were speaking with someone face to face. On the internet, we may feel freer to use profanity and hateful language. We may be quicker to express our anger and disapproval. We may even take pleasure in deliberately leaving hurtful comments on sites and with people or groups we don't like. This is called "trolling."

Really, trolling is nothing but bullying in cyberspace. Its only purpose is to take pleasure in upsetting or picking on other people (for more on bullying, see "Bullying," page 75).

However, we don't have to be trolling to act like a troll. One common dickish mistake is to reduce people to stereotypes in order to dismiss or invalidate what they have to say. This is lazy and presumptive.

Perhaps it should go without saying, but when commenting, never use hurtful slurs, epithets, profanity, or offensive slang. This is never okay. Telling people how wrong they are in the most offensive way possible is "slagging." In truth, this type of behavior only reveals our own ignorance of people who are different from us.

If you find yourself the target of online bullying, slagging, or trolling, there are a few things you can do. First, get help. Tell someone what is going on, so you are not dealing with this alone. Then, ignore the poster if you can. If it's someone approaching you through social media, try to hide or block that person. Above all, do not get in a "flame war" with someone. You'll just get burned.

A Note on Addiction

Social media and the internet should enhance our lives, not become our lives. Admittedly, holding the world in your hands can be distracting. All that information, all those videos, all those photobomb memes!

These are hilarious, but it can be annoying when people become so distracted by their devices that they don't pay any attention to you. If you find people have no idea what you're talking about because your only topic of conversation is funny online videos, you're on the internet too much.

As a courtesy, be sure to put your phone away in the following situations:

When you are out with friends.

When you are out to dinner.

When you are in a movie theater.

When you are in a work meeting.

When you are having a conversation.

And during important life moments.

WHEN IT COMES TO ADULT ENTERTAINMENT

When they say you can find anything on the internet, they mean it! Sometimes an innocent internet search turns up more than you bargained for.

Now, adult entertainment doesn't just show up by accident. Sometimes people really are interested in watching "the birds and the bees" online. And that's okay. The birds and the bees are completely natural. But we should also be careful not to bring our private viewing habits out in public.

So, as a courtesy, be sure to put away any sensitive materials in the following situations:

When you are out with friends.

When you are out to dinner.

When you are at a movie theater.

When you are in a work meeting.

When you are having a conversation.

And during important life moments.

If you share a computer, tablet, or smartphone, and if you accidentally open websites with adult content, don't just close those websites and walk away. Clear the browsing history as well as the browser's cookies for the next person who may use your computer.

Sexting

For adults in a romantic relationship, sending sexy messages and photos can be a lot of fun. However, as with anything involving the internet or social media, the same rules apply: Any text or image that's sent can potentially live in cyberspace forever. In addition, the sender has no way to stop the receiver from posting or forwarding the content to someone else. So play it safe and keep things private.

This is meant for me, and I'm going to keep it for me.

If you are tempted to send a personal photo, stop to consider the potential consequences. Many a politician, celebrity, professional athlete, teacher, and police officer have had their reputations ruined or lost their jobs because they sent indiscreet photos of themselves. So think twice about what you send and whom you send it to.

I respect myself, and don't need to send pictures of my ding dong to strangers for attention.

When Dating Online

The internet has made it easier than ever to find that special someone. The available choices have thus expanded far beyond your job, school, church, drug store, or grocery store. You can choose from millions of people from all over the world!

These days, plenty of dating sites help you focus your search for Mr. or Ms. Right. Maybe you want to find someone who shares your religion, interests, or occupation, or is in your age group. Research the sites and find one that works for you.

> For cheese log aficionados and dog lovers?! Sign me up!

Be Honest

Just like in real life, be yourself and you won't go wrong. Dating sites ask you to create an "online profile." This isn't an avatar of all the qualities you wish you had. It's meant to be you, so be honest! Do not just write down what you think other people want to hear.

> Oh, I don't want to seem too needy. Let's just put "casual" down! I'm a laid-back guy!

If you do, you may find yourself sifting through all the wrong people, and you are likely to be severely disappointed.

> Why are you wearing a tuxedo? I thought you said you were "laid-back"?

It's important to present yourself and your interests clearly to avoid any confusion and a lot of wasted dates.

Use a Realistic Picture

For your online profile, you may be tempted to use the best photo of yourself ever taken. Just remember: Eventually, your date will meet you in person. If the photo of you wearing that sailor costume is from ten years ago, you will now look somewhat different.

Ideally, you want to find someone who will be attracted to you for the person you really are. That doesn't mean you shouldn't polish yourself up a little. It shows you're making an effort. Not too glitzy, and not too dowdy. A good choice is a photo that reflects your personality and interests.

Slow Your Roll

The ability to meet so many people online also means you can date many more people. With the right profile, it's easy to schedule a date every day. This might sound fun at first, but it's exhausting. With so many people to fit in, you never have time to get to know someone. You may find yourself stuck in the same question-and-answer routine.

Where are you from? Oh, that's interesting. What do you do? Oh, cool. What are you favorite movies? Oh, yeah. Uh-huh.

This is boring and not fair to your dates. How would you feel if you found out your date went on five other dates that week? That person might not being taking your date seriously, right? At the very least, it shows that you are not being selective. Remember, you don't have to say yes to everyone.

OK, I'm going to politely decline these people, as I see we have no common interests.

If you're looking for a serious relationship, be serious about choosing your dates wisely. Weed out the people you are not really into. Just like you, those people would rather go on a date with people who are interested in them, not people who are just filling up their free night with whomever they can find. Do them the favor of not wasting their time. Honesty is the best policy!

Now, Don't Be a Dick!

In conclusion, remember: No one is perfect. We all do dickish things now and then. The important thing is to learn from any mistakes and try not to be a dick as much as possible. Focus on doing your best. Be proud of who you are and who you are becoming, and help others to do the same. We each have our own unique insights, talents, and traditions. Every day we can contribute something positive to the world. All you have to do is follow the Golden Rule: Treat others the same way you'd like to be treated yourself!

APPENDIX

A Typology of Dicks

What to Watch Out For

There are plenty of dicks out there, and they come in all shapes and sizes. If you notice someone—or maybe even yourself—conforming to any of the following types, or displaying any of the following behaviors, then you know you're dealing with a dick. And recognizing dick-ishness in action is the first step toward minimizing the overall impact of dickishness in the world.

This list is intended as a brief introduction to the types of dickish behavior you're most likely to encounter in your daily life. But be aware: This list is not compre-hensive. (Not by a long shot . . .)

The Bully

Bullies make fun of other people for what they see as "flaws" and exploit these flaws in order to make *them-selves* feel better. Some bullies grow up and become repentant everyday citizens, while others double down on this bad behavior and be-come talk show radio hosts, supervillians, stand-up comics, etc.

The Elitist

Elitism isn't about having a lot of money or education. It's ignorance about the benefits of privilege and the institutionalized eco-nomic disparities between social classes. It's assuming that poor people must be lazy and stupid or else they wouldn't be poor. It's also assuming that you are a better person just because you have more money, a better job, or a boat.

The Martyr

We all have problems, but martyrs revel in those problems and use them as a sort of emotional capital. By insisting that their lives are awful but hey, you gotta do what you gotta do, martyrs seek to attract attention and draw out compliments.

I don't deserve to be in a relationship. I'm too complex.

The Narcissist

All of us have our moments of narcissism, but a true narcissist is someone who is vain and self-interested to the point of megalomania. Narcissists wind up imposing on others even when they are not treating people with outright disdain. Narcissists are careless at best and destructive at worst.

Selfie! Selfie! Selfie!

The Drama Queen

Being a drama queen has nothing to do with wearing a crown. It's what happens when we lose perspective and treat every bump in the road like it's a mountain to climb. Some people think their lives aren't interesting if they aren't constantly struggling with important "problems"—even if they fabricate those problems themselves.

PROSTITUTION WHORE. You stole my favorite pencil!

The Bigot

A bigot is one who makes generalizations based on other people's race, religion, gender, or sexual orientation. Bigots don't take the time to get to know a person individually but instead rely on their preconceived ideas of what someone should be.

I get confused when people aren't exactly like me.

The Sexist

Sexists believe that one sex is inherently superior or inferior to the other. Sexists also tend to think that each gender has an inherent role, like breadwinner or dishwasher, and that a person's worth is based on fulfilling that role. Sexists not only look down on people of the opposite sex, but their own sex as well.

The Manipulator

Manipulators act as though they have the capacity to directly influence people and events. This is presumptuous and rude and can also lead to a lot of really messy personality conflicts if the manipulator gains a real foothold in a given community. Manipulators are most prevalent on the reality television circuit, but they also pop up regularly in schoolyards, city halls, boardrooms, and fantasy epics on premium cable.

The Passive-Aggressive

As with narcissism, we're all passive aggressive at some point or another. But a dickish level of passive aggressiveness is achieved when someone *consistently* operates via implication rather than direct address. Passive-aggressives are unpredictable, and their lack of communication skills makes it unclear who they are, in fact, really mad at. It's funny from a distance, but awful from up close.